ARE YOU ANGRY, LOST, AND FORGOTTEN! IF SO THIS BEAUTFUL JOURNAL IS DEDICATED TO YOU....

In that caring personal dedication, please know every page in this book has been lovingly written and prayed over in the desire that through these guiding insights, you will find what you need INSIDE! And as you Find the way to Stop being Angry all the time, this book also wants you to find the way to never feel Lost, Alone, or Forgotten in life. Then as you realize that this Universal Journal was written just for You to share..... year by year, you will know somebody out there... Really Does Care!

That's why, with You looking for a way to feel better about YOU as you find a way to survive your current Bad attitude. Knowing right now you are full of Fear, Anxiety, Terror, Stress, and Depression. Likewise, with most of the Whole World feeling Lost, Alone, Forgotten, Frustrated, and Overwhelmed about Everything. To know Somebody out there does Care about Your life, Please read on! Because to find the Best of What Time brings... You need to CHANGE YOUR MIND about a lot of things!

Of note: In this book (that's part of... THE 7 BOOK... AND NOBODY CARES SERIES) .... you will find CARING THOUGHTS TO HELP GET YOU THROUGH THE FALLS IN YOUR LIFE. Likewise, you will see even though these insights cover September, also October. No matter when you read these ORIGINAL, ONE-OF-A-KIND insights, these Universal Daily Merry Thoughts will help you every day of your life!

SEPTEMBER 1.

Do you think that Anybody Out There Really Cares if you feel Angry, Lost, Forgotten? Well in that clue to know somebody does care; you must realize... Life is Not all about you! That means to find who cares for you, you must care for other people too. Then as you show others that you care for them, they will care for you. And when you understand that other people also feel Angry, Lost, Forgotten and Confused. With you wanting to help them. Then you will care more about how They are feeling too. Next being there for them, you will feel better about You. So, as the seasons fall in line, realizing that time will change your life. To make sure everybody around the World cares about each other. Just know that Nobody needs to feel Angry, Lost, Forgotten or Confused because there will always be somebody out there to help them make it through! That's why, doing what Jesus wants us to do. Knowing that Jesus is taking care of me and you... Everybody will find a way to be kind, helpful, compassionate, understanding, and tender hearted to all who they know, meet, and greet. Yes that helpful clue includes finding a way for You...to be nicer to You. Now to keep you from feeling angry, lost, and forgotten in life, also to prove somebody does care all the time. please read these lines found in this personally researched, highlighted scripture that will change your life.. (1 Peter 4:10)

2. To survive the Pain and to find your safe place you must remember when Satan puts you in harm's way, God will always be your refuge, and your strength night and day. That means as your anger, stress, and depression appear. To end the tension that Satan has been building inside of you over the years. To release you from Evil's incarceration, and the Demons manipulations, God will forever be your help in times of trouble as Heaven dry's your tears. Yes, that's good to know, because realizing that Satan is temporarily in control of the world. In life there will be trouble. You will have problems. Your world will be reduced to rubble. But take heart because Jesus Christ Has overcome the Evil in this world. That's why, to make sure your anger, and fear Disappear, knowing Jesus will rebuild what Satan devastates, and takes away. Year after year with you no longer feeling lost or forgotten. That sheltering, Heavenly renovating truth needs to be clear. Because in Faith there is No Fear... only an exciting rearrangement and a great new Beginning that's coming near. Now to prove to you that somebody does care all of the time, please read this personally researched, highlighted scripture that will change your life. (John 16:33)

3. To find a safe place where you can Survive the Floods of Trouble that keep haunting your days also nights and keep bursting your bubble. You need to find the sanctuary in your mind that will bring you relief. That's why to find security as you see things clearly, you must look into the Mirror Of Your Life. Next, as you realize that flood water reflects what your eyes see. You will know that the state of your heart, and the look on your face will determine how you keep handling things. That means to be somebody who can make it through the Frightening sights and Survive the hard times in life, you must look into your heart and see through the Mirror of your Mind. Then trusting Jesus Christ to rebuild your life. By placing a smile on your face, you will find strength in your heart, soul, and mind. Please read this personally researched scripture that goes with this uplifting thought. (Proverbs 27:19.)

4. With you laboring and feeling like your work does not matter, do you feel stressed? Next needing to end your depression, do you know, that no matter what job you are doing... your work is important! So, to do the best job you can in every way.... as you work for the Lord... Not for man. You need to realize it's not what you do, it's how you do it, and Who you do it for.. that's part of the grand, Go Ahead successful plan. So, when you understand that you are working for the Lord. That new work ethic will give you a Shield of Defense from your discouragement. Highlighted by (Colossians 3:23.)

5. In life you need to remember, when your treasures become trash, nothing on earth lasts. That's why, to never be upset over your treasures becoming trash. You need to find your riches in the hope of today and promise of tomorrow that will last. Then finding the way to be happy even when Satan takes your treasures away. You will realize by Not letting your life become trash as you find your Heavenly Treasure that will always last. When you know that renewing times will soon be coming your way that's when you will uncover the best in the day. So, realizing all treasure on earth will eventually be taken away, or become trash. To survive the disasters, you must build up and store your Treasures in Heaven. Yes that restorative insight, will always be the only safe way to think about earthly things that will Never last! So, knowing things will be restored that recuperative truth will always be good news for everybody whose earthly treasure becomes trash. Furthermore, by realizing nobody can take your Hope or Heavenly Treasure away. You will find where your happy heart stays that's where your Soul's Treasure will remain. Therefore, shore to shore, knowing happiness and Salvation will always be the only wealth you will ever need, that joyous priceless revelation will give you the strength to restore your treasure... now and throughout Eternity. Highlighted by (Matthew 6:20.)

6. To understand the difference between mourning, Morning, heartache, and Faith you must realize when you find yourself in Times Of Trouble you will need an escape. Therefore, to find your release from grief. You need to comprehend, to end your mourning and get up the next morning, you must see the differences in many things. That means, you must know in your soul when you Stop mourning to survive your storms, that your tomorrow will arrive with the rainbow. So, to find the way to escape your sorrow. Also to find the way to fill your Present, and Tomorrow with faith, hope, also rainbows.

Please leave your anger, fear, uncertainty, negativity, and your confusing Mourning in the past. Then finding your recovering strength that will last. As you end your storms and start each day with a song in your heart. You will see when you release your grief, and find your great new start... By replacing Heartache with Faith.... there will Never be any mourning in the morning that will tear your world apart. Highlighted by (Psalm 59:16.)

7. Have you found yourself in times of trouble. Have you ever been in a Flood, Fire, Hurt-icane, or Torn-ado that caused a lot of rubble? And knowing you needed a way to survive the pain. With hope fading and no way to go on. Have you ever wondered while feeling weak, will there ever be a way for you to be strong! So, knowing when the flood waters recede, AFTER Satan's devastation is complete.... that the flowers seed that refused to die will start to breathe one more time. Like the resuscitated rose, as you grow, and thrive. You will see when you refuse to cry. By finding your fortification inside, you will never be shaken or Eternally die. Then in your inner strength you will realize once your trouble is through, like the rejuvenated rose greeting the morning dew. By trusting Jesus Christ to tend your soul, like the flowers seed, you will be able to grow, bloom, and start over again too. Highlighted by (Psalm 62:2)

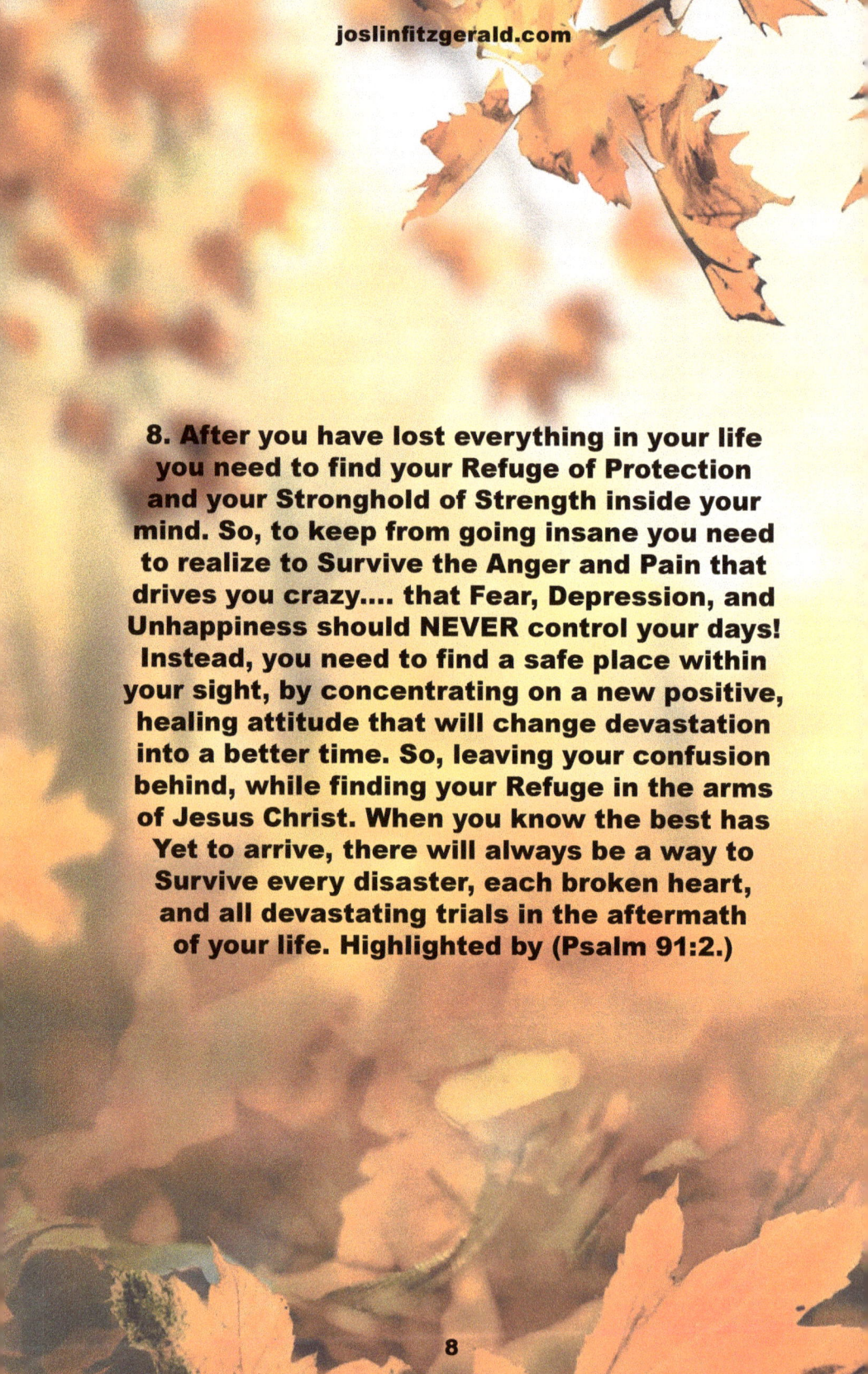

8. After you have lost everything in your life you need to find your Refuge of Protection and your Stronghold of Strength inside your mind. So, to keep from going insane you need to realize to Survive the Anger and Pain that drives you crazy.... that Fear, Depression, and Unhappiness should NEVER control your days! Instead, you need to find a safe place within your sight, by concentrating on a new positive, healing attitude that will change devastation into a better time. So, leaving your confusion behind, while finding your Refuge in the arms of Jesus Christ. When you know the best has Yet to arrive, there will always be a way to Survive every disaster, each broken heart, and all devastating trials in the aftermath of your life. Highlighted by (Psalm 91:2.)

9. Is there is a way to end your discouragement and escape Satan's problems and Pain? Yes there is... and all you have to do is call out Jesus Christ's Name. So, never being dismayed, after finding your strength, while leaning on your Faith. You will realize that anger, anxiety, stress, depression, and pain will eventually go away. That means being held up by the Lords righteous, guiding, healing arms and loving hands, you will find the renewed strength you need to end your desolation and sadness. Please read, (Isaiah 41:10.)

10. Have you ever felt like you are falling? Have you ever wanted somebody to catch you and keep you safe? Well, to stay out of harm's pathway and to keep your heart safe you need to pass your tests today. Additionally, to survive the mess, you must learn from your mistakes. Then to find a way to stay protected and to keep from falling before you run out of time. You will realize, as you learn the way to Survive The Facts of Life Jesus Christ will get you through all the evil attacks, harms, alarms, and the hard times in your life. Highlighted by (Psalm 121:7.)

11. In life there will be times when everybody thinks about living or dying. So, like it or not, we must constantly be talking about Pain, Destruction, Anger, and Devastation that will always be leading you to your Demise or Awakening. That's why realizing any time could be a Day of Pain. In that demise or Awakening situation, we always have to think about how we can Survive the Days of Annihilation. Therefore, shore to shore, in the same way we need to talk about dying before you can understand living. That means to appreciate living, YOU SHOULD NOT LIVE YOUR LIFE LIKE YOU ARE DYING! INSTEAD, YOU SHOULD LIVE... WHILE KNOWING YOU ARE ETERNALLY ALIVE. So, no matter what Pain Satan brings into your days or night.... ENJOY YOUR TIME WHILE CELEBRATING LIFE. Bottom line, Do NOT focus on the pain, fear, anger, destruction, or devastation in your sight that will make you cry. Do Not live like an entombed Flower or a cremated rose who will never see the light. Instead, realize in your healing, awakening, and Change there will always be Light and Survival coming with the sunrise of the next day. So, whether you be living or dying that is good to know, because even though everyone will walk through the valley of the shadow of death, nobody will fear any Evil, since the Lord will always be with us wherever we go. And that Awakening will end all of Satan's destruction, and devastation. Yes that's more good news, because the Gift of Heaven's Love that will always be leading us to the Promise of Everlasting Life above, will now and forevermore bring us peace and comfort today and also tomorrow. Now to keep you from feeling angry, lost, and forgotten in life, also to prove somebody does care all the time please read these lines found in this personally researched, highlighted scripture that will change your life. (Psalm 23:4.)

12. To understand why tragedies happen, also to know why ordinary days and boring seasons can turn into Nights of Fright, Days of Danger, also Times of Extinction, we need to remember that Temporarily Satan is in control of the world's terminal, dying, sick condition. That means the Demons are orchestrating the globe's demolition, terror, agony, and this continuing horror show. But take heart because if you know JESUS CHRIST...SATAN IS NOT IN CONTROL OF YOUR LIFE OR SOUL! So, to understand the ending and beginning you must know that no matter what happens in your time there will be a beauty in your life that arrives. And that's great to know because as Satan Try's to Hurt you. And Hell TRIES, to take your sanity away. To make sure that you don't feel angry, lost, or forgotten night or day. The Lord will give you Peace and Safety that Stays! So, on your ordinary day when SATAN brings devastation, fears, tears, and obliteration your way. Do not let your heart be troubled. Do not be discouraged. Do Not Be afraid. Do not be depressed. Do not be stressed. Because when you have Faith that things will get better... then Satan will never be able to take away your peace, joy, or happiness. Highlighted by (John 14:27)

13. What does the last call, and no warning at all, mean to your life overall? Also, what will happen if during the LAST CALL THERE IS NO WARNING AT ALL that comes your way? So, realizing that all known problems, and unseen troubles are the Teachers of Life. As life teaches you the difference between crying and smiling. Remember when Satan's hard times arrive, as you keep learning from your changing life lessons, that all have to do with survival. ... Jesus Christ will always be your Defense also Strength, and ever-present help in times of problems or trouble. Please read (Psalm 46:1.)

14. To make the change you need inside. Remember the End of Everything on Earth will really just be the Heavenly Beginning for anybody who has Salvation's Rebirth written into their After Life. So, to find your Lifeline always know... that God so Loves the world that he gave his only begotten Son that whosoever believeth in Jesus Christ should not perish but WILL have everlasting life! Yes that Eternal Promise will always be good to know, because as the end comes, with No Warning At All. Knowing you will Not be a part of Hells Last call, sent in the Final Bomb or Fireball. Knowing one day or night you will be on your way to Paradise. You will be glad you won't have to worry about the end of things... that WILL come with No WARNING AT ALL. Highlighted by (John 3:16.)

15. To get through life you must stop playing games. That means you must never trust or depend on what you think, do, or say. Instead, knowing life is not a game, you must have Faith that Jesus Christ knows the way. Next to make sense of the games you keep playing, you need to let the guiding steadfast Love of Jesus Christ direct your seasons... That means, to succeed, you must know that Jesus will never let you lose, fall, or fail. Yes that's guiding insight, because as you see your blessings become new every morning and every night. In Heaven's faithfulness to you and Your Trust in Jesus. You will realize when you let Jesus Christ lead your way by not losing your mind, or resting place. Realizing life is Not a game. After you stop playing games while never doing things your way... your goals, dreams and Heavenly destination will be waiting. Please read (Lamentations 3:21.)

16. Now wondering about the games you are playing. Is the game of life really a game? Or is it possible life is not a game that can be played! And being afraid you can't play the game, while not knowing what games you are playing, those are all guiding insights into how you manage the things happening in your life. That's why, to avoid losing, remember as you play the games of life, you won't win the games you play, if you think life is a game! So, Stop playing your games! And as, you let Jesus Christ lead the way, every day you'll feel like a winner at work or play. So, knowing life is not a game that can be played. In everything you do be Strong, and Courageous. Do not be played. Do not be dismayed. And to be happy.... stop playing your games. Highlighted by (Joshua 1:9.)

17. Knowing that life is Not a game, how can you be on the winning victorious team if you don't know why you keep playing the losing games, you keep playing. And if life is not a game, that's something else you need to know that has to do with your Soul going over the rainbow or going below. That's why, to know if you are succeeding. Next to be on the victorious team, you need to know how to pick the winning Heavenly Side BEFORE you run out of nights and days. That means, knowing that life is not a game to play. To be happy that you won't lose the games you keep trying to play. You need to put your defeatist attitudes behind you. Next to know that victory will never come in the games you play, since life is not a game. Realizing Victory comes in Jesus Christ's name. You will realize that Faith wisdom, and Grace will make you a winner every night and day. Highlighted by (1 Corinthians 15:57.)

18. To stop the devastation and survive the fire you must put out the flames. To take disappointment away you need to realize that life is not a game. To keep your head above water, you must learn how to swim through the flood. To fix the problems that caused you to have a broken heart you need to find a new, happier ending by understanding where your problems started. Then knowing when you Don't feel angry, lost, or forgotten that you can survive the hard times in life. Likewise, realizing by having Faith, your trouble and pain will be rectified. You need to move forward by learning from your decisions, while fixing your mistakes. Next understanding what went wrong at the start...to stop crying, you need to leave the past's broken parts behind. And as you face the things you need to know, but refuse to see, you will find by ending your fear, and stopping your sorrow that Jesus Christ will fill your life with Courage, also other hopeful healing things that will help you cope. And as Jesus gets you through the attack on your soul, that rescued insight will make things better today, tonight, also tomorrow.... That means, while trusting Jesus Christ to put out Hell's fire, and to keep your head above water, as Jesus heals your broken heart when you trust Jesus Christ with your life. You will find Surviving the hard times, will always be easy if you don't fall apart! Please read this personally researched scripture that goes with this uplifting thought. (Isaiah 43:18.)

19. As you make your own plans that keep going astray, you need to stop making your own decisions that will take you the wrong way. Additionally, as you try to make your plans and follow your own directions, you need to realize by trying to do everything Your Way... you will always be going down the wrong highway. That's why, trying to do everything yourself, knowing you are full of doubt... you will only have yourself to blame when your directions don't work out. So, knowing that You Cannot do things on your own. That's when you will see, you need Jesus Christ making the decisions in your life that will make you happy now, and that will take you on the right trip to Paradise for all Eternity. Yes that's great Heavenly Reservation Information, because with all things created through God, for God, and of God. Knowing God was before anything else. As God holds You, and all creation together... Realizing You are Not in control. That means when you learn who has sent you in the right direction, you will also know through God, that our Savior Jesus Christ... has already made your Heavenly Reservation that will one day, or night take you back home, over the rainbow to Paradise.. Now to keep you from feeling angry, lost, and forgotten in life, Please read this personally researched scripture that goes with this uplifting thought. (Colossians 1:17.)

20. As the seasons of your heart beats keep passing you by. To survive the Changes in your life that have to do with the Wild Frightening Sights coming your way. You must realize to get you where you need to be going, things have to Change! That means, with Satan temporarily in control of the nights and days even if change brings heart ache, fear, tears, desolation, and pain... If you keep trusting Jesus Christ to take you the right way...Change will always be a good thing as long as you enjoy your time, by having fun living your life.... Bottom line, to get where you need to be going you must remember that there will always be a time to cry and laugh. A time to grieve and dance. A time to be quiet and a time to speak. A time to be hurt and a time to heal. Likewise, there will Eternally be a time to Live, die, fry or Fly. That's why, to Survive the Wild Frightening Sights of Life that will all change everything in their time. Day and Night while going in the right direction to your final Heavenly Destination, it will always be nice to realize on your away back home to Paradise... To Everything there will be a Sweet Season and a Nice Time under Heaven. Now to prove to you somebody does care all the time, please read this personally researched, highlighted scripture that will change your life. (Ecclesiastes 3:1.)

21. To understand the seasons and to survive the Twisting Winds Within that keep blowing through your life. As the days and nights join together to affect or infect you at work or play. You need to realize The Twisting Wind Within will Change everything in every way. That's why, as you try to Survive the Twisting Winds Within, you need to realize how you manage those changes will always have to do with what remains of life! That means, being fearful or Peaceful... Untroubled, or Afraid... will always have everything to do with where The Twisting Winds Within and The Season of Life take you as you go along your way! Therefore, shore to shore, what you are doing, also where you are going... depends on if you See Change as a good or bad thing. So, to understand The Seasons of Life, you need to find the way to Survive The Twisting Winds of Time! And as the clock stops and starts, with the things you see wasting away, while the unseen things stay. You need to know as old becomes new again, that those Beautiful Heavenly guiding truths will Change Everything. Yes those insights will even tame the Twisting Wind Within your heart, soul, and mind! Now to keep you from feeling angry, lost, and forgotten in life, also to prove somebody does care, please read these lines found in this personally researched, highlighted scripture that will change your life. (2 Corinthians 4:16.)

22. Have you ever thought about the flipside of life? And taking your mind in that switching direction. With your days and nights flipping everything around. As life turns the seasons upside down. Knowing there will always be a change in time arriving. Have you ever noticed, with Everything going out of Control... that the times in your life... have always been Teaching you something that you need to know. And as things keep rotating, flipping, and switching in that teaching realignment. Have you likewise verified in that alteration of time that there will always be a Flipside to Life! That's why knowing Things Will Always Be Turning Upside Down and going out of Control. To Never feel angry, lost, forgotten or alone. You need to realize if you are to Survive the Flipside of Life, as you live, even though you will die. As things flip and switch, to enjoy the Winds of Time, a lot of things need to be rearranged before you run out of sight. So, with time going out of Control, knowing right now you are on the Flipside of life. That means, as you keep following the RIGHT Teaching Signs that lead to renovation, and revelation. Knowing Jesus Christ will always be taking you in the right Heavenly direction. You will finally be able to embrace life's nice flipside of time night and day. Now to prove to you that somebody does care all the time, please read this personally researched, highlighted scripture that will change your life. (John 11:25.)

23. As we think about how time keeps changing life. Realizing everything happening in life will always be about changes, and time. Not knowing WHAT TIME IT IS, or when THE Time Will Be, or when THE TIME arriving will end everything. Likewise realizing Change and Time will always be on our mind. Seeing the leaves leaving the trees, with everything and everybody running out of time. Are you wondering if there will ever be a way to dry your tears as the year keeps getting closer to the Finish line! So, knowing you want to end your fears. Not wanting you to fear Time! Likewise, not wanting you to be Afraid of Change. You need to be on guard and alert while realizing that the rise and fall of time will never be far behind. So, to Never see Time... or Change... as Frightening things. I think we will each agree that everything will always be about the Changes in Time, that will soon be arriving. That's why, not knowing when Time will be Changing, or What time it is. To Never fear time and instead to embrace change. Likewise, to see Time as a friendly part of your journey. Remember as long as you don't run out of time. And you keep trusting Jesus Christ with your life...a Change in Time... will always be a good part of your life's story. Now to keep you from feeling angry, lost, and forgotten in life, Please read this personally researched scripture that goes with this uplifting thought. (Mark 13:33.)

24. As you keep traveling through life with you feeling angry, lost, and forgotten is there a way to keep things from going south? Likewise with things not turning out, have you ever wondered on the dead-end Rocky Road that you are on, what you are doing wrong? So, to keep things from going South Listen to what the Lord is saying. That way, as you follow the right guiding signs, while staying on the straight route, you will always be following the desirable path. Then putting your thoughts away, while listening to what Jesus has to say. The Lord will point out the Divine HIGHway by leading you in truth and inspiration as you go along your way. Likewise with Jesus Christ teaching you wisdom, while guiding you in love, you will always be going in the right direction! Please read, (Psalm 25:4.)

25. Have you ever wondered if you are doing things right? Likewise, have you questioned where you will be heading when the light turns into night? And knowing one day, you will lose sight in your eyes. Those are all important Ending and Beginning inquiries that have everything to do with going the right way in life. That's why to see if things are beginning or ending, you have to know your stops along the line... are really just Starts In Time... that will always get you where you need to be going. So, to Never Fear your Ends or Beginnings. Next to find Strength even when you feel weak and afraid. To receive the Help, you need, and to get you where you are going, you must realize Jesus Christ will always be with you at the end... and in the Beginning of the night or day. Highlighted by (Matthew 28:20.)

26. Is Time your Enemy or Friend? Well that all depends on how You Treat Time as you are going around the bend. So, to make sure Time will always be your Friend! Don't treat time like it is an Enemy!! Instead look Forward to the time that is... as you also look Forward to the time that has yet to be. That way, by not dreading time, you won't worry about your wrinkles, face, age, weight, shape, the weather, your dreams, goals, Future History, or Past mistakes. Yes that's a great thing, because knowing none of that matters in the end. Realizing because of Jesus Christ.... Time will always be your Friend. Time will never be your Enemy! Bottom line, verifying the best in your time has not yet been. Life will never be your enemy.....and Time will always be your Friend! Please read (2 Corinthians 6:2.)

27. In a world running out of time. Realizing unless you change your mind that some of you will be left behind. Are you aware that nobody knows the day or night when Jesus Christ will arrive for the Second time! So, as the weather changes, and the seasons turn into nightmares or sweet dreams. Overnight, you too must be ready for the End of The Line. That's why, to Survive the Facts of Life, you should not concentrate on things that you desire or buy. Instead, to Never run out of time, and to find the way to smile all the time, seek Not the way to stay on earth's side. But instead find the way to NOT be left behind crying... by focusing on keeping your Soul Alive. Highlighted by (Matthew 24:36.)

28. Do Not let fear or pain change your day or night. Remember when you live in Faith, Frightening things will soon fade away. That means, when you find security inside your mind, the bad times will be out of your sight. So instead of being fearful or frightened by time .... focus on what's Nice in life. Then as you change your mind and turn fright into a smile. You will find by changing the way you see things that the bad thoughts and destructive times will leave your vision and mind. Next as you go through life smiling. You will realize that sunset to sunrise, year after year... by Not Living In Fear, no matter what terror or fright, Satan brings into your life. Shore to shore, Jesus Christ will keep your soul safe from all harm and alarm forevermore. Please read (Psalm 121:7.)

29. Is your life full of indecisions and time lapses? Are you fearing the aftermath of the crash? If so, not wanting you to fear the repercussions of Satan's latest disaster. You need to know to keep your soul whole, that you must give Jesus Christ... The Time... to rebuild what Satan destroys. Then Never Fearing Tomorrow also Never being Afraid of the morning... you must look for your pain, danger, and devastation to change. And as, you trust Jesus to pick up Satan's pieces. By finding the best that comes your way you must let the bad thoughts and frightening times leave your mind night and day. And as you trust in your Faith that things will get better with Time. To keep you whole, also sane, you need to allow Jesus Christ.... The Time.... to pick up your broken pieces along the way. Highlighted by (Proverbs 3:5.)

30. Have you ever listened to the sweet comforting breeze? And wanting you to slow down, while sending you a Calming message that will bring peace into your life. Have you ever listened to The gentle song of the Seasons that will change your timeline! So, knowing listening to the friendly sweet comforting breeze will always be a reassuring thing. To take a mental vacation from life you need to realize that listening to the sweet reassuring message of time will continuously be a great way to take a rest from your tests, stress, problems, and trials. That means, listening to The sweet breeze dancing through the flowers, as the breeze kisses the trees. That mental relief will always be a good thing for your soul, mind, and also body. Because the message of love coming from above found in the sweet song of the seasons, will give you a mental break as it tells you every day... Don't Fear or Worry about ANYTHING. Bottom line, never fear, or worry about the frightening, unsettling things happening on earth that come your way. So, instead of focusing on the bad times, find the Nice things in your sight. Enjoy your days and nights. Appreciate Life. And as you verify that Jesus Christ has given you everything Good in life! Praise the Lord your God with all your heart, all your soul, and all your might... now and until the end of time. Then finding Serenity in your life. You will see all you have to do to be content inside your soul, and mind... Is LISTEN! Yes LISTEN to the gentle song of the Seasons. And as you also LISTEN to what Jesus keeps saying as Heaven talks to you through the Peace In The Breeze... then you will find your happiness that will never leave. Highlighted by (Matthew 22:37.)

October 1.

To get the sweet treat you must be able to survive the sick trick! Yes that's nice insider advice that will help you find the best things in life. And that Guiding treat will always be necessary, because as harvest starts, as fall calls, while Halloween plays its haunted part. I think we will each agree that overall things are getting sweetly interesting, and or equally sick and tricky. That's why, to survive the aftermath of The sick trick you need to find the Sweet treat in all the seasons. That means, as life Haunts you, to find the Guidance that will take away Satan's misleading sick tricks, you must end Hell's taunting crippling lies, and stop falling for the Demons deceits. Bottom line, as time keeps flying by, always remember as Jesus Christ's face shines on you in the mornings light, that the Gracious Sweet Treat of Heavenly Guidance.... will forevermore be in your sight. Now to keep you from feeling angry, lost, and forgotten also to prove somebody does care all the time, please read these lines found in this personally researched, highlighted scripture that will change your life. (Numbers 6:25)

2. In our time that keeps passing by, while finding what we need, most of us have been happy, and fulfilled also appreciative about what we have received. But with some of you entangled in your empty seasons trying to get what you should not have. Instead of being happy with what you have been given.... you have been trapped in dissatisfying, frightening times because you have not accepted what you need. So, being unhappy and discontented, Remember, what you want will not always be good for you, but receiving what you Need will complete and fulfill you. Yes those are insightful thoughts about want and need that will get you what you want, and what you Need to Receive. That's why, to never be Angry in a Tricky Situation, or Lost in a Haunted Season, or Forgotten in a Blind Time, you need to take the disappointing frustrating times out of your life. Then replacing Satan's tricks of want, desire, dissatisfaction, and unfulfillment .... with Heavens gifts of fulfillment, contentment, completion, and the Sweet Treat of Paradise that you Need to Receive... You will find the Sweet Serenity of God's peace, and Heavenly appreciation that transcends all understanding will guard your heart and mind through Jesus Christ. That means... Salvation will give you Everything you will ever need!... Now to prove to you that somebody does care all the time, please read this personally researched, divine scripture that will change your life. (Philippians 4:7.)

3. Are you aware that pain and Satan have many names. Likewise, are you aware that Satan can be seen in many faces. Additionally, do you know that Satan will show up in many places. So, knowing that Satan will be found in many places, since Satan has many names, and faces. Verifying that Placement statement to be true. To Defeat your fear and to live in peace. Do Not be afraid of your day. Do Not be afraid of people's faces. Do Not be afraid of going places. Do Not be afraid of Life. Bottom line, to turn your back on Fear, be Strong and Courageous while trusting everything will be alright. So, in review, to be free to live your life. Don't be Afraid! Likewise, Do not be discouraged. Do Not be dismayed. For the Lord, your God will be with you wherever you go to tomorrow also today. So, realizing Jesus Christ will always be by your side. Likewise knowing Jesus already defeated Satan and stopped Evil. You will realize that even though Satan has many names also faces, and Evil will be found in a lot of places. Knowing everything will work out fine, you Won't be afraid of living your life. please read these lines found in this personally researched, highlighted scripture that will change your life. (Joshua 1:9.)

4. Have you ever felt angry, lost, forgotten, alone and defeated? Have you ever felt like the only leaf left on the tree? Well, that's not the way life should be! But with some of you Not knowing how life should be. With you feeling left behind in Times season. That means you keep feeling displaced along the way. And with you barely hanging onto your Family Tree, you need to know..... that is not the way life should be!! So, remember even though there may be nobody home. And even though you may have no friends or family. Additionally, even though you are alone... There Is A Way TO NEVER BE LONELY! Because day and night Jesus Christ will always be there to be your Best Friend in life. And as, Jesus gives you the sun and moon to light your way. Jesus will always give you comfort and beauty night and day. That means as, Jesus Christ gives you the birds who fly by to say Hi. And as, Jesus gives you the rainbows also following blue skies to make you smile. Just as Jesus sends his Angels to watch over you day and night. Even though you may Feel like the only LONELY leaf left behind on the tree ... As long as you Praise Jesus Christ from the rising of the sun to the setting of the moonlight.... Knowing that springtime will arrive. Soon your Life Tree will be filled with the best things in time including friends and family. So, knowing better days are on their way you won't ever need to feel angry, lost, alone, defeated or forgotten in your life night or day. Highlighted by (Psalm 113:3.)

5. Do you know where you will be gathering, and what will you be harvesting? So, to answer that receiving question and to be somebody who appreciates what they reap from the seeds of wisdom that have been planted in their field. Likewise, to be someone who enjoys their spiritual harvest and who knows the reason to show appreciation for what they have received. Always being a smart person who understands Who they want to be. Likewise, to see, who you are becoming... You need to know that gathering insight has nothing to do with Halloween, corn, wheat, rice, or beans. Instead, Who you are, and Who you want to be, has everything to do with Planting and Harvesting what your Soul Needs! That means, Knowing Who you are, and where you will be Eternally gathering, as you Celebrate the Sweet Treat fact that Jesus Christ will help get you through all Satan's trials in your life. Knowing that Jesus Christ has prepared your Heavenly gathering place. As Jesus has already prepared a place for you in Paradise. In the great Harvest of Souls that will soon be arriving...By accepting your Salvation, while praising Jesus Christ with all your mind and heart while being glad and rejoicing... that will always be the best part of the harvest. Please read this personally researched verse that goes with this uplifting thought. (Psalm 9:2.)

6. To stop the following black shadow of evil that's dark as night, you need to eliminate the doubtful, sneaky, creepy things that Haunt your life... So, instead of living in fear of darkness, turn away from the Sneaky Seasons of the Demons. Then turning your back on Evil and other creepy things in life... Let your HEAVENLY light shine. Don't let Evil fool or conquer you. Don't let Fear or Misery rule you. Don't let Unhappiness or Stress Stop you. And as you replace your life of anger, anxiety, and dread, with Smiles and Laughter instead. By looking ahead to the sweet times. You will stop seeing through the Demon's Eyes. Then smiling inside, you will make it through the Creepy times. So, to depart from anger... find Laughter. To Never feel forgotten or be lost... find the Cross. Then having a released, free, quiet mind cling tightly to the things that are nice and right in your sight. Please read, (Psalm 34:14.)

7. To know if you are doing Halloween, time, and life right, you must see what's Right in front of your eyes. Next, to See things clearly, you need to stop letting others Scare, Trick, and Frighten you into doing the wrong things that you should Not do. So, instead of doing things the wrong way, make the wise choices and the right decisions every day. Then you will see by doing what's right, that Heavenly Wisdom will watch over you, and Jesus Christ's guidance will preserve you. Next, understanding you... are doing things the Right way, that Heavenly knowledge will protect your eyes. And as, truth guards your heart night and day, the right decisions in life will keep you safe. Highlighted by (Proverbs 2:11.)

8. Do you know the difference between a trick and treat? Yes that's something else you need to know if you don't want to be tricked, trapped or to be unhappy. So, to receive the treat... and to keep from being tricked or trapped you need to know the difference between the future and the past. That means to locate the way to make half and half whole, when life seems broken also hollow you need to seek the way to escape the disturbing things that are bothering you. That's why, to find the way to make a trick a treat, you must know the difference between being trapped or being released. And as you find peace in your life, and a safe place in your mind, always be joyful day and night. Never stop Praying, Praising, or Celebrating Jesus Christ for all the good and nice things he keeps bringing into your life! Bottom line, to be free from Satan's anger, loss, and tricky times, be thankful in all circumstances of your life. Likewise Rejoice always knowing that soon you will be released from your trap. Next to never feel forgotten or lost, and always be seen... that's good advice. Because in your escape from Satan's tricky trap, there will constantly be beauty and also enlightenment when you get out of your frightening ensnared deception and find the Heavenly Difference between a Trick and Treat. Now to prove to you that somebody does care all the time. please read this personally researched, divine scripture that will change your life. (1 Thessalonians 5:16.)

9. In life it will always be important to see the difference in everything. That's particularly important when you are thinking about the difference in tricks and treats. Because the difference between a trick or treat will always be.... that one is comforting, fulfilling and also sweet. But the other tricky part will always be full of emptiness, agony, and misery. So, when you are stuck in the middle of a big decision put the tricks and uncertainty behind you. Then find the smart sweet things in life that fulfill you. And as you lean on Jesus for everything, remember the Lord gives wisdom and insight through His Divine words. Likewise, from His mouth Jesus Christ gives knowledge. And from His protective daily enlightenments Jesus Christ gives love, and guidance. That means, as you Understand how to survive Satan's sick tricks and tricky traps in life you need to find Jesus Christ. Then, as you realize Jesus will help you end your emptiness, also escape your misery, by getting you through your uncertainty, and agony. You will also see that Jesus Christ will always be the only sweet fulfilling Treat that you will ever need now and throughout Eternity. Highlighted by (Proverbs 2:6.)

10. So, knowing that right now many of you feel like you are caught in a tricky trap. Have you also ever felt like you are behind the door in a dark jail cell living in a continuing nightmare? Then trapped in your Anger, while feeling Lost also forgotten have you ever wondered if there will ever be a way out. Next unable to sleep have you ever felt like sweet dreams don't exist? Well, knowing you are Not the only one who feels that trapped, defeated, tricked way, remember it only takes one smile, or kind word, or nice gesture to change a life today! That's why, Never knowing what trap, depression, grief, or stress.... You... or somebody else are in... a smile, nice gesture, or a kind word will let everybody INCLUDING YOU...know someone cares about them. So, to find the escape you need from all your depression and grief. Remember just as Lord releases you from Satan's dark jail cell and takes your nightmares away by freeing you from your mental incarceration. Jesus Christ will turn your darkness into light. Then making sure that no harm, no sickness, no nightmares haunt you Jesus will put his Angles in charge of protecting your soul. Now to prove to you that somebody does care all the time, please read this personally researched, divine scripture that will change your life. (Psalm 91:10)

11. The sweet treats in life will always be easy to find if you slow down and take your time. So, to avoid the icky sick tricks and to stay Out of the tricky traps don't take the wrong path. Next to be released from your stinky decisions don't let your earthly rotten thoughts guide you. Instead listen to what Jesus tells you to do. Then when you make smarter choices Jesus Christ will make sure you stay on the right track. So, when Jesus Christ says... Go Forward and Walk this Right way... listen to what Jesus shares with you today. Because, that will be your Soul's inner voice, telling you the right things to say, the right things to do, the right way to think, and the right way to Go along the way too. Please read (Isaiah 30:21)

12. To know if you are going the right way you must know which way you are heading today. So, knowing that Jesus knows the correct way for you to go. Acknowledge Jesus Christ's direction and His Heavenly decisions every day. Then trust with all your Soul that Jesus will direct your path in the right way! Next, by trusting in the Lord with all your mind and heart, as Jesus Christ lights your road in life every night and day. Know in Faith that you are going the right way! And as you End your Anger, to Never feel Lost or Forgotten, you will find the way to end your Frustrations. Then allowing Jesus Christ to lead you down the right road. By living in Faith not in Fear.... Year after year you will NEVER be carrying the weight of the world on your shoulders! Highlighted by (Psalm 25:4)

13. On the wild ride that we call life... IS everything really all about what You think, say, do, share, and write? Or WAIT! Are these same life changing things about what Others think, say, do, write, share, and know too. Bottom line is making sure that You are Saved, all about what I am doing to help you? Or is Sharing, the Caring Present of Salvation... important for you to do for Others too? Yes that's more guiding light insight. Because NOT Everything Is About You! That means, sharing the good news about Jesus Christ with others, will always be important too! That's why, to make sure Everybody Survives The Facts Of Life, we must all find the way to survive the spooky, frightening Tricky Traps of Time. So, To keep someone's Soul breathing. Like me, You too, must Share The Lord's healing and guiding words all over the world with everybody. And as, you share the Caring Love of Jesus Christ with those in your life, or those you meet on a blog, or pass on the street... don't judge them, also don't treat anybody cruelly, or with ridicule. Instead, be kind, and tender hearted also compassionate to one another just as Jesus has been Forgiving, Loving, and Caring to you. Please read this personally researched scripture that goes with this uplifting thought. (Ephesians 4:32.)

14. Have you ever questioned what season you are in? Then feeling like you will always be frozen in time. Will it always be wintertime within your heart, Soul, and mind! Then being weak when you need to be strong. Have you ever felt like a discarded leaf that's dying inside while Frozen in Time! So, Not knowing where you will be landing, while feeling that way night and day. I know that right now there are some of you feeling weak, frightened, Frozen in Time, and Afraid. That's why, to find your Strength inside you need to stop feeling like a dying leaf, and instead see yourself as an Evergreen. Then being Strong when you feel weak, while being Courageous when you feel discouraged, your winter will turn into spring. Then the Hail of Pain, also the cold desolation in your soul, will be over. And as your life's blizzard and tornado turns into a rainbow... you will stop crying. Likewise, you will stop dying inside. Next as you learn to be Courageous by trusting Jesus Christ for everything wherever you go. You will find your Strength inside your heart, mind, also soul. That's when, no longer feeling angry, lost, alone, Frozen in Time, or forgotten... by being Strong When You Cannot be Weak, you will be complete. Then being Courageous when you feel Discouraged... you will realize no matter what time or season it is in your life, because you have found your Strength within with Jesus Christ... it will always feel like an Eternal springtime. Highlighted by (Joshua 1:9.)

15. To stop living in the past that should not last, quit living in your black depressing hollow hole. Also Stop wishing life might be what it was not meant to become. Next to find your peace, let life be what it is meant to be one day and night after one. Then always knowing your sunrises and sunsets will get better as time goes by. Remember the past will constantly be full of sad, hollow, painful, horrifying, Tricky Trap black holes that must be Left Behind! But the Good News will always be, when you leave the Tricky Trapped past behind...and live in Faith... knowing things will soon get better, your Present will be full of sweet times also happy places. So, to find happiness today, DO NOT FALL into your Black Past's Tricky Trap Hole that holds painful memories, regrets, or sorrows that are OVER! And instead of living inside your past's sad black hole.... enjoy the whole, beauty, Joy, and Peace of your Present day, while looking forward to the Hope of Tomorrow! Yes indeed to enjoy your happy place get out of your past's dark black painful hole and let today be a whole Sweet Treat full of goals and potential. Happily, those new possibilities are wide open, since today will Always be the way to Start Over! Now to keep you from feeling angry, lost, and forgotten, please read this personally researched, highlighted scripture that will change your life. (Romans 15:13.)

16. So, wondering what will happen to you after a BOMB IN YOUR HEART GOES OFF. While realizing in life there will always be Many Different Kinds of Bombs that will break your body and crack your heart. Next, knowing to find a new start... that you need to survive the pain, fears, and tears in life after the torpedoes launch. As you Survive the Bombs of your Heart, that will go off! To get your new Start knowing some BOMBS will physically go off, as Others will figuratively blow up your heart. Realizing in different ways Bombs will drop and torpedoes will launch. To End your Fear, and no longer feel lost, or alone year after year. You must realize to Survive Satan's Bombs that will Rip you Apart ...You need to find the quiet gentleness in your mind that comes from trusting Jesus Christ with every part of your days and nights. Bottom line, to survive the after math of the torpedoes that will launch, including the BOMB of your Heart.. that will go off. You need to realize inside Jesus Christ's arms, will always be the only place for you to find peace in your life ... That's why, when the bombs drop, to never fall apart, you must love Jesus Christ with all your heart, soul, might, also mind. Highlighted by (Matthew 22:37.)

17. Now still thinking about Satan's Bombs that Drop, attached to a Pain that leads to broken hearts. Wanting you to be able to start over and not fall apart. After the BOMB GOES OFF do you know how to make a new start? Well, to survive the fallout when the BOMB GOES OFF and you need a New Start... you must know even when your plans die... if you are peaceful and calm inside, you will always know deep down in your soul, if you keep trying to find the best times in life... things will eventually be alright. Likewise, finding a new start after the BOMB IN YOUR HEART GOES OFF means even though you feel like you are dying inside, as you keep your dreams in sight, that your hopes, goals, and desires will also stay alive. Yes that's good to know, because as the Lord blesses you, and keeps you, as the Lord lifts you up, and is gracious unto you. You will see even when Satan Drops a Bomb on your Heart, and Evil Rips your Life Apart. By knowing that things will work out right. There will always be a way to get a new start. Bottom line, even when Satan's Bomb Drops...you will find by following Jesus Christ's guidance, when things seem their darkest in the night, there will always be a Heavenly light ahead that will change your life! Highlighted by (Numbers 6:24.)

18. Are you Still thinking about your haunted past, and things that should not last. Well to make sure that you are not Haunted by the painful past or caught in History's Tricky Trap... here's some more guiding advice.. KEEP THE PAST IN THE PAST! Next DON'T LET THE PAST RUIN YOUR LIFE! Bottom line, DON'T LET THE PAST LAST! And to make sure the Past Does Not Last, remember to be happy today The Pain In The Past Must Go Away. So, even though the ghostly Haunted past will be a taunted part of the trip of life that's going by way to fast. Going forward in different ways, Jesus Christ will fill you with Joy, Hope, and Peace tomorrow also today. That means to find what's new as, you trust Jesus to end your depression, also to take away your sorrow, and frights... Jesus Christ will guide your way to a better life! That's why, to find what makes you happy today, you must not let your Treacherous Haunted Past get in your way! Likewise, you must not allow yesterday's Past Tricky Traps fool you into thinking they are your new today... or your future. Bottom line, to get out of your disheartening Tricky Traps, find what's nice, new, and happy in your life! And to do that... Don't let the bad, frightening, ghostly Haunted Past last! Highlighted by (Isaiah 43:18.)

19. Are you living in an unhappy haunted house of doubt. Are you possessed by your tricky trap past? Well, knowing that some of you are caught in that Past trap. To get out of your Unhappy Haunted House of Doubt, you need to be released from the previous misery that keeps following you around. That means, to Never be Possessed by your Haunted Past you need to be good, caring, truthful and nice to YOU, while leaving your Tricky Trapped History behind. Then finding the good times today, life will figure itself out no matter what you have already done, seen, known, or have said along the way...That's why, to be HAPPY today you need to know as you grow and Survive Satan's Bombs of the Heart that WILL DROP.... To end your PAST HAUNTING, and to GET OUT OF TODAY'S TRICKY TRAP... You must remember that right now Jesus Christ has healing plans to prosper you, and not harm you! Likewise, Jesus plans to fill your life with hope and an amazing future. So, knowing you Can survive the Bombs of the Dark World that will drop. Likewise realizing that you Can survive the Torpedoes of the Heart that will launch. That's when you will realize, as Jesus Christ brings your Present, and a great tomorrow to you .... To Stop Your Haunting Thoughts that should not last! By being happy today and Happier tomorrow you can leave the Unhappy bad PAST IN THE PAST! Highlighted by (Jeremiah 29:11)

20. Do you know that the difference between Hello and Hell No... is in coming and going. Do you also know that the inSINerating Horrifying fire in Hell is real! Or WAIT! Is telling you living without Jesus Christ in your life, while you go to Hell and Fry alive for all time... just a way to lie to you, also to steal your good times, and to tell you how you should feel. Bottom line is telling you, living without Jesus Christ ... just an icky trick to keep you from having insight in your life. Or is HELL'S HORRIFYING FIRE REALLY REAL? Well with all of us seeing what HELL CAN BE as we are going through our personal Hells in life, or as we keep seeing glimpses of Hell on our TV...I will tell you personally after Going Through Hell many times...that Hell IS THE REAL DEAL...That's why, to Survive the icky tricks that will make you Eternally Sick... if you don't believe Hell is real for your soul.... To stay out the Horrifying Hellish FIRE below. Likewise, to avoid the ETERNAL PAIN, you must NOT try to find out if Hell is the Real Deal Before you Die, Run Out of Time. And instead, you Must face the fact HELL will be HORRIFYING when you die!.. So, to Never go into the Hellish Fire, and instead head to your righteous Delightful Eternal life, Don't turn your back on Jesus Christ. Highlighted by (Matthew 25:46)

21. Have you ever wondered if you will be able to survive the trick that makes you sick or cry? So, knowing there is only one way to avoid the trick that will make you sick inside, and cry outside. You must turn away from the things that Haunt you. Likewise, you must change the times that Taunt you and bring Fear into your life. That's why, to smile all the time, you must remember the Trick in Life is not in living... BUT THE TREAT IS IN LIVING RIGHT! So, as night is gone, as the new day dawns. To free your mind and leave the tricky times behind. Turn away from the darkness in your life. Next to keep smiling, change the way you look at things. And to live life right... put on the Armor of Eternal Light, that has been given to you by Jesus Christ. Please read, (Romans 13:12.)

22. Are you wondering who keeps playing tricks on you? Well guess what, that trickster and clueless one is YOU! Yes, You are the one Playing Tricks on YOU! So, to stop playing foolish sick tricks in your life, seek the Peace and Joy you need to find. Next to find your serenity inside, stay away from the tricky icky sick thoughts in your mind that cause you to doubt your future. Then no longer being troubled, or afraid you will be able to Stop feeling confused, lost, forgotten also Enraged. Bottom line, Don't let Satan fool or trick you. And instead of being clueless, find Insight. Next Replace life's sick tricks with Heavenly treats. Then you will find the contentment, joy, also tranquility you seek and need. Highlighted by (John 14:27.)

23. Can a trick make you sick? Well to answer that question, and to make sure you avoid the sick tricks you keep playing on yourself. The answer is Yes, a trick can make you sick. So, to stay healthy, stop tricking your mind into thinking things are fine. And instead of falling for the Evil Trick that will make you Sick, find the Heavenly Treat that will renew you while that healing blessing repairs what's inside. Then not being sick inside your soul or mind. That Gift of Today's Strength, and the Present of your future's enlightenment, will make you healthy and wise. Bottom line, when you understand it's Satan who is breaking you down, while the Demons keep playing their ICKY tricks. Realizing life, and Satan will make you weak and sick! That's when you will appreciate, there is a way to heal and recuperate from the sick tricks that Satan plays. Yes that's great recovering news today. Because when you heal the Mental Pain that tricks your mind night and day. That's when, you will see Your strength, refuge, and safe place will always be waiting behind the Shield of Jesus Christ's words that have been given in Heavens Present of the PRESENT, presented in the Divine Gift of the Future, which are all contained within Jesus Christ's healing name. Highlighted by (Psalm 119:114.)

24. To find the truth inside your soul also mind, you must decide if it's a sick trick, or sweet treat that you seek in your life. Then realizing that Satan's distressed sick trick is what makes you sick, leave your fear behind. Do Not let things in the world confuse you. Do Not let Today cause you anxiety. Do not let the Future break your heart. Do Not be tricked. Do Not be perplexed. Do Not let Satan lie to you.. And instead of being mystified, tricked, perplexed, and confused by the demons... Listen to what Heaven wants you to hear. Then let Jesus Christ guide your mind as you find God's, pleasing, truthful, perfect, and peaceful will for your life. Please read, (Romans 12:2.)

25. To protect you from the sick tricks that will be news, you must know what a lie is and what is the truth. That's why, to see through the tricky traps that will hurt you and fill your life with agony, you must turn your back on bad news and grief. To do that... Do Not believe lies. Do Not fall for deception. Do Not fall for the trick that will make your soul sick. And to stop suffering, Only let reliable Divine Good News guide your life. Then following your heart and trusting your soul, you shall know also See... the truth about everything. And that Heavenly Truth will set you free! Highlighted by (John 8:32.)

26. So, knowing as you keep feeling downtrodden and forgotten that you want your lost abandoned reality to change. To hang on, as this out-of-control world spins violently upside down. You must find a way to keep your feet on the ground. Next to stay balanced when everything is falling apart at the seams, before it all blows up, you must find a way to keep from breaking down, also to stop throwing up! Next to keep your heart from breaking apart. And to no longer be lost, and instead to be Happy all the time, even when Satan makes you cry...You must Celebrate the good times that will soon start, BEFORE THEY ARRIVE .... That's why, to End your Anger and to never feel lost, alone, or forgotten, as you cope with what's happening in your life, you need to know that things will get better if you just give them time! So, Do Not be frightened about time passing you by. Do Not cry about anything. And instead of being stressed and depressed... BEFORE THEY HAPPEN... Rejoice over the delightful, comforting things that will soon arrive in your Life. Likewise, BEFORE THE GOOD TIMES ARRIVE... Praise Jesus Christ for your days and nights. Then knowing at all times, since you found the Cross, you will never be lost. You will find the peace that transcends all understanding... will guard your heart, soul, and mind through Jesus Christ. Highlighted by (Philippians 4:4-7.)

27. Are you being taunted and Haunted by Nightmares? Well, knowing that some of you KEEP feeling that spooky way about your nights and days. To stop being Haunted by the upsetting times in life that keep preoccupying your days. You must stand up to the taunting things that keep you up at night! That means, to End your Taunting's, and to STOP your Past Hauntings by changing your troubling attitude. You must do something to fix what is disturbing and distressing you! Then as you understand why you are always being Haunted by your PAST and Taunted by your PRESENT Nightmares. While you take the FUTURE pressure off of your shoulders...Remember you are not going through life alone! That means, by finding your Sweet Dreams there will always be a way for you to let your Hauntings, Taunting's, and Nightmares Go! So, instead of getting upset about everything that keeps happening, Trust in the Lord with all your heart and soul. Know when you go to sleep, you will have No fear or anxiety. Likewise realize when your Past Hauntings Stop that Jesus Christ will make all of your dreams Sweet. Then as Jesus Christ brings you into the Sweet Dream Team, while safely directing your pathway day and night. All the Hauntings from the past and your current Taunting Hallucinations, and delusional Nightmares that ruin your sleep and keep you Awake TODAY... will go away overnight. Highlighted by (Proverbs 3:24.)

28. Now talking about masks. Are you hiding behind your mask of pain? Next silently suffering through Satan's Devastation are you afraid to let people see you cry, and disintegrate? Well, to escape those tears and fears you need to realize A Mask will Not Hide The Sorrow Or Fright In Your Eyes! So, to find happiness in your life, Stop Crying and Take Off Your Mask THAT YOU ARE WEARING INSIDE. Next dry your eyes and let your Smile shine! Then Ending your Anger, while no longer hiding and feeling lost or forgotten Inside, everybody will see the good things going on in your mind. That's why, to heal what's happening inside, and to See Your Smile outside.... Masks Need To Be Removed. Because there is nothing covered up that will Not be revealed to.... and or shared about you! Therefore, since everything Hidden will be Known, also since your soul will be Exposed. Take Off Your Mask that's Hiding what's happening behind your eyes. Don't fear the night. HEAL what's transpiring inside. Then knowing that Satan will NO longer be in control. While trusting Jesus Christ to make things right, after Satan makes you cry and leaves you feeling hollow .... By FOLLOWING JESUS CHRIST, AFTER TAKING OFF YOUR MASK. Let your smile, and the light inside of your soul shine also grow. Now to prove to you that somebody does care all the time, please read this personally researched, divine scripture that will change your life. (Luke 12:2.)

29. Who do you want to be in life? Likewise, whose are you? Yes those are all insightful Why you should be like that, and Who you need to be inquiries, that have to do with every day and night in between. That means, those Who, and Why thoughts will always be Key to Whose you are, and to Who you are meant to be. That's Why, a costume will never be as important as the Kind, Sharing Compassionate, Forgiving, Loving, Caring, Tender hearted, Unmasked person you are MEANT to be... So, let the people See Who you are..... Then because of WHOSE you will always be.... they will like Who they See! Bottom line one more time, Who you want to be, Whose you need to be, also Who you should be, and Why you need to be, will always be connected to the time you spend listening to the words of Jesus .... And as Jesus shows you...HOW TO BE.... Who you are meant to be, Who you will be, and WHOSE you will always be! Take Off Your Mask that you are hiding behind. Next always be the Compassionate, Forgiving, Nice, and Kind person Who you are in life! Then knowing Whose you will be... as you are living and witnessing for Jesus .... everybody will like... what they hear, also What, and Who they see. Highlighted by (Ephesians 4:32.)

30. Please do not terrify the adults or frighten the children! Yes that's great advice ANY day or night. That's why, to be nice to the children outside, we need to remember what it was like for Us when we were once frightened little kids on Halloween night. Bottom line, with all of us knowing that Haunting FRIGHTENING SIGHTS, NIGHTMARES, FEARS, AND TEARS NEVER GO AWAY or LEAVE OUR MIND! As TERRIFIED adults who are STILL Afraid of our Own Shadow... We need to realize no matter our age, We are All STILL Haunted, Horrified kids hiding inside our mind, who are STILL afraid to show our faces! So, to take the gruesome sights out of our eyes, as we calm our minds, and enjoy our life, we each need to find a way to Escape Fright by NEVER letting Terror come Inside! Therefore, shore to shore to Never Let Fear Come Near us, also to Never let Horror HURT the kids... We need to remember to take the fright out of our eyes, and to put the nice things back into the children's days and nights... that we need to be Kind all the time! That's why, no matter our age, Everybody needs to realize... that Gentle, Reassuring, Polite words, and Kind deeds... will always be like honey in our life.. Yes those Nice things will always be Sweet Treats for the soul.. also, equally healing to our body, mind, and our Shadow! Highlighted by (Proverbs 16:24.)

31. To understand the golden rule, and for you to Stop crying over the PAST things that keep Haunting you. You need to Lift Up Your Mask that you keep hiding behind, so you will be able to open your eyes and see things clearly in your life. Then finding the Nice, Kind, Polite person who lives inside of you, by doing to others, as you want them to do unto you too... as they do nice things back to you. Everybody will finally be doing things right. Then with everybody around the world being Nice, Kind, and also Polite to each other, while putting smiles on each other's faces. You will see when you treat others as You want to be treated by ending all Hauntings, YOU WILL FIND Peace Inside your Soul, also Mind. Then Doing Unto Others as you want Them To do UNTO EVERYBODY. By not Frightening the Kids or Terrifying Other adults and Not Hurting you too ... By never being mean, rude, or cruel... everybody will know how to follow the Golden Rule! Now to keep you from feeling Angry, Lost, and Forgotten in life, also to prove somebody does care all the time. Please read these lines found in this personally researched, highlighted scripture that will change your life. (Matthew 7:12.)

So, knowing this is Not the end and it is instead just the Beginning of many good things... As you have read this book and have been blessed with peace, and reassurance. I am praying that you no longer feel Angry, Lost or Forgotten. Likewise, to work through some of your other Negative emotions realizing (to keep the prices down) that this book only covered SEPTEMBER, AND OCTOBER. For more blessings that will take you through the Other Months, please find the following books in this series that have also been produced in beautiful COLOR.

Of NOTE...This book called ANGRY, LOST, and FORGOTTEN.... follows the Fall seasons, and holidays. But like the other SIX books in this line.... that follow their own Holidays, feelings, and Seasons. You will find no matter when you read any of the words in the .... AND NOBODY CARES SERIES ...or THE coming soon AWAY BACK HOME NOVELS. That ALL these Merry Thoughts will Bless your days and nights no matter what day of the year you read them.

For more from Mary Joslin... also known as Author Joslin Fitzgerald... please use these QR CODES...to go to her web sites, and blogs there you will find out more about her 18 CHILDREN'S BOOKS, HOLLYWOOD PROJECTS, MOVIES, and her other writings THAT INSPIRED HER GENRE CHANGE AND GAVE BIRTH TO HER NEW AUTHOR'S NAME!

Information sheet

So, knowing Daily we will all be Celebrating SOMETHING in some-way. Realizing every hour will be something to CELEBRATE. TO FIND THE WAY TO BE HAPPY ALL OF YOUR LIFE. Let's take this time to appreciate the continuing gifts and blessings we have been given. And as, we look forward to the Present of the Todays Present, lets CELEBRATE the Happy Future coming our way.

NOW, TO READ THE POPULAR BLOG CALLED AWAY BACK HOME AND FOLLOW JOSLIN FITZGERALD'S WRITING, TO READ ALONG, PLEASE GO TO JOSLINFITZGERALD.COM

to find out about Joslin Fitzgerald's 18 bestselling children's books, 5 animated movies, Hollywood projects, and the exciting coming soon 15 adventure packed novels please visit her blog and web sites at JOSLINFUN.COM, or ARISINGWRITERS3. BLOGSPOT.COM or ARISINGWRITERS.COM

Published by Circles Legacy Publishing LLC
Book design copyright © 2024
Project Manager and Team Coordinator: Mary Cindell Lynn Pilapil
Cover Design: Jim Villaflores
Layout Coordinator: Joseph Apuhin

Published in the United States of America

ISBN: xxx-x-xxxx-xxxx-x

Adult Inspirational Journal
July 12, 2024

www.ingramcontent.com/pod-product-compliance
Lightning Source LLC
Chambersburg PA
CBHW051558120626
46551CB00013B/1569